LONGEVITY SOLUTION COOKBOOK

LONGEVITY Solution
Cookbook:

Easy-to-Cook Recipes to Help you Live Healthy Through all Seasons.

By

Dave Miller

LONGEVITY SOLUTION COOKBOOK

Copyright © 2019, By *Dave Miller*

ISBN-13: 978-1-950772-92-6
ISBN-10: 1-950772-92-6

All Rights Reserved. No part of this publication may be reproduced in any form or by any means, including scanning, photocopying, or otherwise without prior written permission of the copyright holder.

Disclaimer:

The information provided in this book is designed to provide helpful information on the subjects discussed. The publisher and author are not responsible for any specific health or allergy needs that may require medical supervision and are not liable for any damages or negative consequences from any treatment, action, application or preparation, to any person reading or following the information in this book.

LONGEVITY SOLUTION COOKBOOK

Table of Contents

INTRODUCTION 6
   Secrets to a Healthy, Long Life 6
2. THE TOP DELECTABLE LONGIVITY RECIPES! 8
   Delectable Breakfast recipe 8
   Smoked Salmon & Avocado Hand Rolls 8
   Apple and Horseradish-Glazed Salmon 9
   Feel-Good Salmon Sandwich 10
   Salmon Cakes with Dill Sauce 12
   Maple-Glazed Salmon with Pickled Cucumber 13
   Salmon and Scallop Skewers with Romesco Sauce 15
   Smoked Salmon-Wasabi Tea Sandwiches 17
      Savory Sage and Cheddar Waffles 18
      White Pizza Frittata 20
   Low Carb Mock McGriddle Casserole 22
   Bacon Cheddar Chive Omelets 24
      Bacon Avocado Muffins 25
   Raspberry Brie Grilled Waffles 27
   Pumpkin Spiced French Toast 29
      BBQ Pulled Pork and "Cornbread" Waffles 30
      Blueberry Banana Bread Smoothie 32
      Chicharrons con Huevos 33
      Jalapeno Cheddar Waffles 34

LONGEVITY SOLUTION COOKBOOK

Spinach and Cheddar Scrambled Eggs 35

Delectable Dessert recipes *36*

Raspberry Pavlovas 36

Amaretti Cookies 38

No Bake Coconut Cashew Bars 40

Raspberry Cheesecake Cupcakes 41

Delicious Chocolate Brownies 42

White Chocolate Bark with A Twist 44

Pumpkin Snickerdoodle Cookies 46

Vanilla Cream Cheese Frosting 48

Chai Spice Mug Cake 49

Low Carb Cookie Butter 51

Coconut Peanut Butter Balls 52

Cream Cheese Truffles 53

Delectable Dinner Recipes *54*

Hasselback Marinara Chicken 54

Low Carb Sweet and Sour Meatballs 56

Skillet Browned Chicken with Creamy Greens 58

Spicy Sausage & Cabbage Skillet Melt 60

Reverse Seared Ribeye Steak 61

Chicken Zoodles 62

Cheddar Bacon Explosion 64

General Tso's Chicken 66

Creamy Spinach Pork Tenderloin Roulade 68

Paprika Chicken 70

Low Carb Chicken Satay 71

Baked Sea Bass with Herb Cauliflower Salad 72

Spicy Cauliflower Rice & Salmon Medley 74

Low Carb Sweet and Sour Meatballs 76

LONGEVITY SOLUTION COOKBOOK

    Blackberry Chipotle Chicken Wings 78

    Hearty Crock Pot Chicken Stew 79

Delectable Sides and salad **81**

    Sundried Tomato Tuna Salad *81*

    Tuna Avocado Salad *82*

    Chia Seed Strawberry Jam *83*

    Bacon Cauliflower Mash *85*

    Brussels Sprout Cherry Tomato Salad *86*

    Tuna Salad on Sliced Cucumbers *87*

    Sesame Zucchini Cucumber Salad *88*

Delectable Dip and Spread Recipes **90**

    Paleo Macadamia Nut Pesto Rolls *90*

    Raw Creamy Avocado Pesto *92*

    Parsley-Thyme Spinach Pesto *93*

    Healthy Chicken Nuggets *95*

    Cream of Broccoli Soup" (dairy free) *96*

    Sun-dried Tomato Spread *98*

    Pesto Shrimp and Quinoa Stack *100*

    Coconut Curry Fettucine with Capello's Gluten-free Pasta *101*

    Easy Garlic Baked Cod with Vegetable Medley *103*

    Coconut-Seared Sea Scallops with Raw Kale, Avocado and Salsa *105*

    Mustard Dill Crusted Fish Filets *107*

    Marinated Buffalo NY Strip Steak *108*

    Balsamic Fig Puree *109*

    Steak Salad *110*

    Baked Salmon with Grainy Mustard, Parsley and Sliced Shallots *111*

    Pomegranate-Blueberry Baked Cod *112*

    Pesto *113*

    CONCLUSION *115*

INTRODUCTION

Secrets to a Healthy, Long Life

It is widely known that living a healthy lifestyle enhances good health and a longer life expectancy by incorporating behaviors that improve health into a person's lifestyle while avoiding behaviors that are damaging to one's health.

Diet has been popularly acknowledged as a cornerstone of health and wellness. There is minor doubt that eating natural foods, reducing sugar and avoiding snacks plays a huge role in weight control and metabolic health.

Longevity is not just about increasing lifespan, but instead about enhancing 'health-span'. It's more about quality of life, not total length one has lived. Nobody on earth wants to live with chronic illness and pain. Too little protein is bad, since our bodies depend on getting enough to maintain functionality. But the most asked question is whether too much protein is bad. This is a tricky question, and one that requires a nuanced approach. Until recent years, it was practically considered not possible to eat too much protein. Atkins diet (low carbohydrate diets) recommended low-carbohydrate intakes, but made no specific recommendations about protein or fat intake. When joined with the low-fat mania, people are made to eat a low carbohydrate, low-fat diet – which leave only protein in the diet. This turned out to be very difficult to adhere to. It was highly restrictive and was basically salad, egg whites, and turkey daily.

However, the big differentiation of the older style low-carb diets and the Ketogenic or keto diets is that keto diets allow liberal amounts of fat, and suggest moderation of dietary protein. Excess consumption of protein often kept one out of ketosis if you were eating constantly. During this period, there was the strong belief that we should be eating 6-10 times daily, promoted by many physicians based on no evidence whatsoever. Eating a diet much, much higher in fat allowed ketosis and for some people, it was successful.

Remember, that there are many other nuances in protein intake, too. There is a big gap in animal versus plant proteins. Generally, since we are animals, those proteins are closer to what we require, and have a higher biologic value. Animal proteins are highly nutritious, and the reason why traditional societies spent so much energy on hunting animals, even though for most, their main source of food was plants. This higher nutritive value is great if malnutrition is the problem.

Unfortunately, overnutrition tends to be more of a disaster in recent world. Therefore, the high nutritive value is not always healthy. This pro-growth signal has been associated to many diseases of aging and excessive protein.

THE TOP DELECTABLE LONGIVITY RECIPES!
Delectable Breakfast recipe

Smoked Salmon & Avocado Hand Rolls

Prep Time: 25 minutes

Cook Time: 10 minutes

Tips:

Remember that this salad is full of protein from the salmon and hard-boiled eggs.

However, if you want to cut back on cholesterol, I suggest you avoid the eggs, and you'll still get lots of protein.

Note: protein is rich in omega-3 fatty acids, which studies show play an important role in brain health.

Ingredients

1 ounce of smoked salmon

¼ avocado (mashed)

3 tablespoons of red onion (chopped)

3 nori (seaweed) sheets

One tablespoon of capers

¾ cup of cooked and cooled brown rice

3 slices of tomato

Directions:

1. First, you spread avocado on nori sheets.
2. After which you top avocado with salmon, onion, brown rice, tomato, and capers; roll up nori sheets.

LONGEVITY SOLUTION COOKBOOK

Apple and Horseradish-Glazed Salmon

Tips:

Remember that there is no raw seafood in this roll, so even those who avoid sushi for that reason can enjoy this.

However, to save time, use the brown rice that you batch-cooked earlier in the week, or use a precooked variety.

Ingredients

1 tablespoon of champagne vinegar

2 teaspoons of olive oil

2 tablespoons of prepared horseradish

¼ teaspoon of freshly ground black pepper

1 tablespoon of finely chopped fresh chives

4 (6-ounce) salmon fillets (about 1 inch thick), skinned

1/3 cup of apple jelly

½ teaspoon of kosher salt (divided)

Directions:

1. Meanwhile, you heat oven to 350°.
2. After which you combine apple jelly, chives, horseradish, vinegar, and ¼ teaspoon salt, stirring well with a whisk.
3. After that, you sprinkle salmon with ¼ teaspoon salt and pepper.
4. Then you heat oil in a large nonstick skillet over medium heat.
5. At this point, you add salmon, and cook 3 minutes.
6. Furthermore, you turn salmon over; brush with half of apple mixture.
7. After that, you wrap handle of skillet with foil; bake at 350° for 5 minutes or until fish flakes easily when tested with a fork.
8. Finally, you brush with remaining apple mixture.

LONGEVITY SOLUTION COOKBOOK

Feel-Good Salmon Sandwich

Tips:

Although this recipe is high in fat, salmon and olives are rich in unsaturated fats, which are proven to help heart health.

Ingredients

2 tablespoons of grated Parmesan cheese

1 teaspoon of Spanish smoked paprika

¼ teaspoon of black pepper

4 radicchio leaves

1 garlic clove

Dash of salt

¼ teaspoon of salt

4 toasted whole-grain rolls

¼ cup of toasted walnuts

1 tablespoon of extra-virgin olive oil

¼ teaspoon of crushed red pepper

1 ½ teaspoons of olive oil

1 (about 6-ounce) package fresh baby spinach

1 tablespoon of fresh lemon juice

1 teaspoon of dark brown sugar

4 (6-ounce) salmon fillets

Directions:

1. First, you put spinach, garlic clove, walnuts, Parmesan cheese, lemon juice, 1 tablespoon olive oil, and a dash of salt into a food processor; pulse, scraping down sides of bowl, until smooth.
2. After which you transfer the pesto to a bowl; cover and chill.

3. After that, you combine paprika, dark brown sugar, crushed red pepper, ¼ teaspoon salt, and black pepper in a small bowl.
4. Then you pat dry salmon fillets; sprinkle tops with spice mixture.
5. At this point, you heat 1 ½ teaspoons olive oil in a nonstick skillet over medium-high heat.
6. Furthermore, you reduce heat to medium; cook fish 7 minutes on both sides or until golden and cooked through.
7. After that, you split rolls in half; spread 1 tablespoon pesto on each bottom, and top with 1 fillet and 1 radicchio leaf.
8. Finally, you add tops of rolls and serve with extra pesto.

Salmon Cakes with Dill Sauce

Ingredients

4 large egg whites (divided)

1 tablespoon of fresh lemon juice

2 cups of leftover salmon (broken into pieces)

¾ cup of panko (Japanese breadcrumbs)

½ cup of sliced cucumbers

1 ¼ cups of leftover wheat berries

1 cup (about 2%) Greek-style yogurt

4 teaspoons of pickled ginger

½ cup of whole-wheat breadcrumbs

¼ cup of chopped fresh dill

Directions:

1. First, you mix wheat berries, salmon, whole-wheat breadcrumbs, and 3 egg whites.
2. After which you form into 8 patties; chill for 15 minutes.
3. After that, you dip cakes in remaining egg white and dredge in panko.
4. Meanwhile, you heat oven to 425°.
5. At this point, you combine yogurt, dill, and lemon juice; set aside.
6. Furthermore, you bake salmon cakes in middle of oven for 15 minutes or until heated through and tops are golden.
7. Meanwhile, you heat broiler; brown tops of cakes for about 10–20 seconds.
8. Finally, you serve with pickled ginger, cucumbers, and dill sauce.

LONGEVITY SOLUTION COOKBOOK

Maple-Glazed Salmon with Pickled Cucumber

Ingredients

½ small red onion (sliced)

¼ teaspoon of black pepper

2 teaspoons of grainy mustard

1 cup of seasoned rice vinegar

1 fennel bulb (thinly sliced)

Olive oil cooking spray

1 garlic clove (minced)

¼ cup of sugar

1 teaspoon of olive oil

1 pound of skinless salmon fillet

¼ teaspoon of ground cumin

1 English cucumber (thinly sliced)

¼ teaspoon of salt

1 ½ tablespoons of pure maple syrup

Directions:

1. First, you combine vinegar and sugar in a saucepan; bring to a boil.
2. After which you simmer 5 minutes or until sugar dissolves.
3. After that, you add cucumber and onion.
4. Then you cool to room temperature, stirring, 25 minutes.
5. At this point, you remove the vegetables with a slotted spoon; place in a bowl.
6. Furthermore, you add fennel and olive oil, tossing to combine.
7. This is when you season with salt and pepper.

Directions for Preheat broiler.

1. First, you line a shallow baking pan with foil; coat lightly with olive oil cooking spray.
2. After which you arrange the salmon in a single layer on the pan.
3. After that, you combine the maple syrup and remaining ingredients; spread onto salmon.
4. Then you broil salmon for 6 minutes or until just cooked through.
5. This is when you portion into 4 servings.
6. Finally, you divide the salad among 4 plates; top with salmon.

Salmon and Scallop Skewers with Romesco Sauce

Prep Time: 20 minutes

Cook Time: 6 minutes

Yield: Makes 4 servings (serving size: 2 skewers and 3 tablespoons romesco sauce)

Ingredients

3 tablespoons of fresh lime juice

1 red onion (cut into 1-inch chunks)

1 tablespoon (about 8–9 almonds) of coarsely chopped blanched almonds

2 tablespoons of extra-virgin olive oil

2 tablespoons of extra-virgin olive oil (plus additional for brushing grill)

1 (about 8-ounce) salmon fillet cut into 8 equal pieces

One red bell pepper (cut into 1-inch chunks)

¼ teaspoon of kosher salt

8 ounces sea scallops (about 8 scallops)

1 poblano chile (cut into 1-inch chunks)

¾ cup of drained bottled roasted red bell peppers (chopped)

¼ teaspoon of freshly ground black pepper

¼ teaspoon of freshly ground black pepper

8 (about 8-inch) wooden skewers (soaked in water for at least 1 hour)

Romesco Sauce

½ cup of cherry tomatoes (roasted)

¼ teaspoon of kosher salt

2 garlic cloves (coarsely chopped)

1 tablespoon of sherry vinegar

Directions:

1. Meanwhile, you heat grill or grill pan.
2. After which in a baking dish, you combine kosher salt, lime juice, extra-virgin olive oil (plus additional for brushing grill) and ground black pepper (through lime juice).
3. After that, you add salmon and scallops to dish, and stir with a wooden spoon to coat all pieces.
4. Then you cover and refrigerate for about 10 minutes.

Directions for the Romesco Sauce:

1. First, you process the almonds and garlic in a blender until coarsely chopped.
2. After which you add the roasted red bell peppers, cherry tomatoes, olive oil, 1 teaspoon hot water, and sherry vinegar, blending until smooth and scraping down the sides, if necessary.
3. After that, you season with the salt and pepper, and set aside.
4. Then you remove the salmon and scallops from the marinade, and discard liquid.
5. At this point, you pat dry each scallop and chunk of fish with paper towels (NOTE: This will let the outside get crisp.)
6. Furthermore, you thread each wooden skewer lengthwise with scallops, salmon, onion, red bell pepper, and poblano chile pieces.
7. After that, you lightly brush grill rack or grill pan with oil.
8. This is when you cook skewers over indirect heat 2–3 minutes, then turn gently so that the fish doesn't break and fall into the fire. (NOTE: Use a vegetable or fish basket makes it easier.)
9. Then you continue to cook 2 minutes more or until salmon feels firm to the touch and scallops show light grill marks.
10. In addition, you remove skewers from grill or grill pan.
11. Finally, you arrange 2 skewers on each plate, and spoon the Romesco Sauce over them, or pile the skewers on a serving platter and serve the Romesco Sauce on the side.

Make sure you serve immediately.

Smoked Salmon-Wasabi Tea Sandwiches

Prep Time: 15 minutes

Yield: Makes 4 servings (serving size: 2 sandwiches)

Ingredients

8 slices very thin white bread (crusts removed)

½ avocado (pitted and chopped)

4 thin slices red onion

½ teaspoon of wasabi paste

1 ½ tablespoons of each of chopped fresh chives, sesame seeds, and wasabi sesame seeds (such as Roland)

1 tablespoon of fresh lime juice

2 ounces of thinly sliced smoked salmon

Directions:

1. First, you combine avocado, wasabi, and lime juice; mash with a fork until smooth.
2. After which you spread 1 tablespoon avocado mixture on 4 bread slices.
3. After that, you top with smoked salmon and red onion.
4. Then you top with 4 remaining bread slices; cut in half diagonally to form triangles.
5. At this point, you spread one side of shorter edge of triangle with avocado mixture; dip edge into chives or sesame seeds, pressing to coat.
6. Finally, you transfer to a platter; serve immediately.

Savory Sage and Cheddar Waffles

Ingredients:

½ teaspoon of salt

2 eggs

1 1/3 cup of coconut flour (sifted)

¼ teaspoon of garlic powder

3 Tablespoons of coconut oil (melted)

3 teaspoons of baking powder

2 cups of canned coconut milk

1 cup of shredded cheddar cheese

1 teaspoon of dried ground sage

½ cup of water

Directions:

1. First, you heat your waffle iron according to manufacturer's directions, at a moderate heat.
2. After which in a mixing bowl whisk together flour, baking powder, and seasonings.
3. After that, you add liquid ingredients, then stir until stiff batter forms.
4. Then you mix in the cheese.
5. At this point, you liberally grease top and bottom panels of the waffle iron, then place a 1/3-cup scoop of batter onto each iron section.
6. This is when you close the iron and cook until steam rises from the machine and the top panel opens freely without sticking to

the waffle. (NOTE: proper cooking usually takes 2 cycles at moderate heat.)

White Pizza Frittata

Note: this makes a total of 8 servings of White Pizza Frittata.

Ingredients:

5 oz. of Mozzarella Cheese

4 tablespoons of Olive Oil

12 large Eggs

1 teaspoon of Minced Garlic

¼ teaspoon of Nutmeg

9oz bag of Frozen Spinach

½ cup of Fresh Ricotta Cheese

Salt and Pepper (to Taste)

1 oz. of Pepperoni

½ cup of Parmesan Cheese

Directions:

1. First, you microwave frozen spinach for 3-4 minutes.
2. After which you squeeze the spinach with your hands and drain off as much water as you can; set aside.
3. Meanwhile, you heat oven to 375F.
4. After that, you mix together all of the eggs, olive oil, and spices.
5. Then add in the ricotta, parmesan, and spinach. (NOTE: when adding the spinach, break it apart into small pieces.)
6. At this point, you pour the mixture into a cast iron skillet, then sprinkle mozzarella cheese over the top.
7. This is when you add pepperoni on top of that.

8. Finally, you bake for 30 minutes. Remove from the oven, slice, and serve!

Low Carb Mock McGriddle Casserole

Note: this makes a total of 8 servings of Low Carb Mock Casserole.

Ingredients:

10 large Eggs

½ teaspoon of Onion Powder

1 cup of Almond Flour

4 oz. Cheese

¼ teaspoon of Sage

¼ cup of Flaxseed Meal

6 tablespoons of Walden Farms Maple Syrup

Salt and Pepper (to Taste)

1 lb. Breakfast Sausage

4 tablespoons of Butter

½ teaspoon of Garlic Powder

Directions:

1. Meanwhile, you heat oven to 350F.
2. After which you put a pan on the stove over medium heat, then add the breakfast sausage. **(NOTE:** break up while it's cooking.)
3. Then, in a separate bowl, measure out all dry ingredients (including cheese), then add the wet ingredients.
4. After that, you add 4 tablespoons of syrup and mix together well.

5. Furthermore, once the sausage is browned and somewhat crispy, add everything (including excess fat) into the mixture and mix again.
6. After which you line a 9x9 casserole dish with parchment paper and then pour the casserole mixture into the dish.
7. At this point, you use 2 tablespoons syrup drizzled over the top for extra maple flavor.
8. This is when you place in the oven and bake for 45-55 minutes.
9. Then, once done, remove from the oven and let cool.
10. Finally, you remove the casserole by holding on to the edges of the parchment paper and lifting out.

Bacon Cheddar Chive Omelets

NOTE: makes 1 serving of Bacon Cheddar Chive Omelets.

Ingredients:

1 oz. of Cheddar Cheese

2 slices Bacon (already cooked)

2 stalks Chives

1 teaspoon of Bacon Fat

Salt and Pepper (to Taste)

2 large Eggs

Directions:

1. First, you make sure all ingredients are prepped.
2. After which you heat a pan on medium-low with bacon fat in.
3. After that, you add the eggs, and season with chives, salt, and pepper.
4. Then, once the edges are starting to set, add your bacon to the center and let cook for about 20-30 seconds.
5. This is when you turn off the stove.
6. Finally, you add the cheese on top of the bacon and fold edges on top of the cheese like a burrito - holding the edges in place to use the cheese as a "glue".
7. Then you flip over and warm through on the other side.

LONGEVITY SOLUTION COOKBOOK

Bacon Avocado Muffins

NOTE: this makes a total of 16 Avocado Bacon Muffins.

Ingredients:

½ cup of Almond Flour

4.5 oz. of Colby Jack Cheese

1 teaspoon of Dried Chives

1 teaspoon of Baking Powder

2 tablespoons of Butter

2 medium Avocados

1 teaspoon of Dried Cilantro

1 ½ tablespoons of Lemon Juice

5 Slices of Bacon

1 ½ tablespoons of Psyllium Husk Powder

1 teaspoon of Minced Garlic

Salt and Pepper (to Taste)

5 large Eggs

¼ cup of Flaxseed Meal

3 medium Spring Onions

¼ teaspoon of Red Chili Flakes

1 ½ cup of coconut Milk (from the carton)

Directions:

1. First, in a bowl, mix together eggs, almond flour, spices, flax, psyllium, coconut milk and lemon juice.
2. After which you leave to sit while you cook the bacon.
3. Then in a pan over medium-low heat, cook the bacon until crisp.
4. After that, you add the butter to the pan when it's almost done the cooking.
5. You chop the spring onions and grate the cheese.
6. At this point, you add the spring onions, cheese, and baking powder; crumble the bacon.
7. This is when you add the crumbled bacon and melted butter to the batter.
8. Furthermore, slice an avocado in half, remove the pit, and then cube the avocado while it's in the shell. (NOTE: Be careful of the sharp knife as you do this.)
9. After that, you scoop out the avocado and fold into the mixture gently.
10. Meanwhile, you heat oven to 350F, measure out batter into a cupcake tray that's been sprayed or greased and bake for about 24-26 minutes. (NOTE: you should have a leftover batter to make 4 more muffins, which you Store in the fridge and enjoy cold!)

Raspberry Brie Grilled Waffles

NOTE: this makes 2 servings of Raspberry Brie Grilled Waffles.

Ingredients:

The Waffles

1 teaspoon of Vanilla Extract

7 drops of liquid Stevia

1/3 cup of Coconut Milk

2 tablespoons of Swerve

2 tablespoons of flaxseed meal

2 large Eggs

½ cup Almond Flour

1 teaspoon of Baking Powder

The Filling

2 tablespoons of Butter

½ cup of Raspberries

1 tablespoon of Swerve

Zest of ½ Lemon

3 oz. of Double Cream Brie

1 tablespoon of Lemon Juice

Directions:

1. First, you mix together all waffle ingredients and then cook on a waffle iron.
2. Then, while warm, lay slices of brie across waffles.

3. After which in a pan, heat butter and swerve.
4. Once browning, you add raspberries and lemon juice/zest.
5. After that, you let this cook until bubbling and jam-like.
6. At this point, you place waffle sides with brie under a broiler until brie is soft and waffle is slightly crisp.
7. Finally, you assemble waffle with brie and raspberry compote.
8. Then you "Grill" in a pan over medium heat for 1-2 minutes per side.

Pumpkin Spiced French Toast

Note: this makes a total of 2 servings.

Ingredients:

½ teaspoon of Vanilla Extract

4 slices of Pumpkin Bread

¼ teaspoon of Pumpkin Pie Spice

1 large Egg

2 tablespoons of Butter

2 tablespoons of Cream

1/8 teaspoon of Orange Extract

Directions:

1. First, you let the bread dry out overnight in open air after you have sliced it.
2. After which you mix together egg, extracts, and pumpkin pie spice.
3. After that, you let the bread soak on both sides in the mixture.
4. Then you heat butter in a pan until almost browned, then add bread slices.
5. This is when you flip when browned and continue to cook until browned on both sides.
6. Finally, you serve with Keto maple syrup and some extra powdered swerve.

BBQ Pulled Pork and "Cornbread" Waffles

NOTE: this makes 4 total servings of 1 waffle and 4oz. of pulled pork.

Ingredients:

½ teaspoon of Salt

2 tablespoons of Golden Flaxseed Meal

¼ cup of BBQ Sauce

1 teaspoon of Baking Powder

3¼ cup of Sour Cream

2 tablespoons of Chopped Red Pepper

1 cup of Almond Flour

2 tablespoons of Butter

¼ cup of Coconut Milk (from carton)

16 oz. of Pulled Pork

large Eggs

1 tablespoon of Psyllium Husk

Directions:

1. First, you make the BBQ Sauce and then make the waffle batter by mixing the wet ingredients into the dry.
2. After which you pour the batter on to the waffle maker and let cook.
3. Then, while cooking, add pork to a pan on medium-low heat with about 3/4 of the BBQ sauce.

4. Finally, once waffles are done, spoon pork onto waffle and top with extra BBQ sauce.
5. Make sure you serve with extra sour cream if you'd like!

Blueberry Banana Bread Smoothie

NOTE: this makes 2 total servings of Blueberry Banana Bread Shake.

Ingredients:

1 tablespoon of Chia Seeds

10 drops of Liquid Stevia

2 tablespoons of MCT oil

¼ teaspoon of Xanthan Gum

3 tablespoons of Golden Flaxseed Meal

2 cups of Vanilla Unsweetened Coconut Milk

¼ cup of Blueberries

1 ½ teaspoons of Banana Extract

Directions:

1. First, you add all ingredients together into a blender. (for me, I prefer to wait a few minutes so that the flax and chia seeds have enough time to soak up some of the moisture.)
2. Then you blend for 1-2 minutes until everything is incorporated well; serve up!

Chicharrons con Huevos

NOTE: this makes 3 total servings of Chicharrons con Huevos.

Ingredients:

1 medium Tomato

Salt and Pepper (to Taste)

1.5 oz. of Pork Rinds

¼ cup of Cilantro (chopped)

5 large Eggs

2 medium Jalapeno Peppers (de-seeded)

4 slices of Bacon

1 medium Avocado

¼ medium Onion

Directions:

1. First, you cook bacon and remove to paper towels for later.
2. After which you keep bacon fat in the pan.
3. After that, you cook pork rinds in bacon fat, then add diced vegetables.
4. Then, once onions are almost translucent, add cilantro and mix together.
5. At this point, you add pre-scrambled eggs, let cook, and stir once.
6. Finally, cube and avocado and fold into the eggs.
7. Enjoy!

Jalapeno Cheddar Waffles

Note: this makes a total of 2 Jalapeno Cheddar Waffles.

Ingredients:

1 teaspoon of Psyllium Husk Powder

Salt and Pepper (to Taste)

1 tablespoon of Coconut Flour

1 small Jalapeno

3 large Eggs

1 oz. of Cheddar Cheese

3 oz. of Cream Cheese

1 teaspoon of Baking Powder

Directions:

1. First, you mix together all ingredients using an immersion blender, until everything is smooth.
2. After which you heat your waffle iron, then pour in the waffle mix. (NOTE: about 5-6 minutes in total.)
3. Finally, you top with your favorite toppings, and serve!

Spinach and Cheddar Scrambled Eggs

Ingredients:

Pinch Pepper

½ Cup of Cheddar Cheese

Pinch Salt

4 Cups of Fresh Spinach

1 Tablespoon of Olive Oil

4 Large Eggs

1 Tablespoon of Heavy Cream

Directions:

1. First, you assemble ingredients together.
2. After which you add your 4 eggs to a cup or bowl.
3. After that, you add 1 tablespoon of heavy cream and salt and pepper to taste.
4. Make sure you mix so there are still egg whites showing.
5. Then you heat a large pan to high with 1tablespoon olive oil
6. At this point, you add your spinach once the oil has reached its smoke point.
7. Furthermore, you add salt and pepper as the spinach begins to sizzle, stirring frequently.
8. Then once the spinach has fully wilted, reduce heat to medium low and add eggs.
9. Finally, you stir slowly once the eggs have set and add your cheese.
10. Once it melted, then you plate and enjoy!

Delectable Dessert recipes

Raspberry Pavlovas
Ingredients:

Base:

2 teaspoons of Xanthan Gum

1 teaspoon of Fresh Lemon Juice

½ cup of Erythritol

4 large Egg Whites

1 teaspoon of Vanilla Extract

Filling:

1 cup of heavy cream

85g Frozen Berries

Topping:

1-2 Mint Leaves

18 Fresh Raspberries

Directions:

1. Meanwhile, you heat oven to 300°F.
2. After which you separate 4 eggs carefully and beat the egg whites until they're foamy.
3. After that, you add in erythritol a little at a time while beating.
4. At this point, you mix until stiff peaks.
5. Then you add in vanilla, lemon juice, and xanthan gum; then fold together with a silicone spatula.

6. Furthermore, you line a baking sheet with parchment paper and use a pencil to outline a cup or bowl to guide you when spooning the pavlova mixture. (NOTE: This recipe makes 6 mini pavlovas about 5 inches in diameter.)
7. After which you spoon the pavlova batter so that it's roughly the size of each circle you've drawn.
8. Using the back of a spoon, create a dip/well in the center for the filling later, then you bake for an hour. (NOTE: The pavlovas should turn a crisp, golden brown.)
9. At this point, while the pavlovas are cooling, I suggest you prepare the filling.
10. Measure out 85g of mixed frozen berries (NOTE: Strawberries, blueberries, and blackberries work well to make a beautiful purple color.)
11. This is the point when you blend with a cup of heavy cream for about 3 minutes so the mixture is thick enough to spoon.
12. Finally, you spoon some of the frozen berry mixtures into each pavlova and top with some fresh berries and mint!

Amaretti Cookies

Ingredients:

¼ teaspoon of Cinnamon

4 tablespoons of Coconut Oil

1 tablespoon of Shredded Coconut

½ teaspoon of Baking Powder

2 large Eggs

2 tablespoons of Sugar-Free Jam

2 tablespoons of Coconut Flour

½ cup of Erythritol

½ teaspoon of Almond Extract

1 cup of Almond Flour

½ teaspoon of Salt

½ teaspoon of Vanilla Extract

Directions:

1. Meanwhile, you heat your oven to 350F.
2. After which you combine all your dry ingredients, then add wet ingredients and combine well.
3. After that, you form your cookies on a parchment paper lined baking sheet.
4. Then you add an indent in the middle of each cookie using your finger.
5. This is when you bake for about 16 minutes or until the cookies turn golden and crack slightly.

6. After which you let cookies cool on a wire rack and add a bit of sugar-free jam to each indent.
7. Finally, you sprinkle some shredded coconut on top of each one and enjoy!

LONGEVITY SOLUTION COOKBOOK

No Bake Coconut Cashew Bars

Note: this makes a total of 8 servings of No Bake Coconut Cashew Bars.

Ingredients:

1 teaspoon of Cinnamon

1 cup of Almond Flour

½ cup of Cashews

¼ cup of Butter (melted)

¼ cup of Shredded Coconut

¼ cup of Sugar-Free Maple Syrup (like Walden's Farms or make your own)

1 pinch of Salt

Directions:

1. First, you combine melted butter and almond flour in a large bowl and combine.
2. After which you add cinnamon, salt, sugar-free maple syrup and shredded coconut; mix well.
3. After that, you roughly chop ½ cup of cashews (you may use raw or roasted) and add it into your coconut cashew bar dough.
4. Then you mix very well again.
5. This is when you line a baking dish with parchment paper and spread the coconut cashew bar dough in an even layer.
6. Finally, you place them in the refrigerator and chill for minimum 2 hours.
7. Once they're chilled, I suggest you slice into bars and enjoy!

Raspberry Cheesecake Cupcakes

Note: this will make 12 total servings that are fluffy and decadent.

Ingredients:

½ cup of Granulated Sweetener (I prefer Stevia)

½ stick (about 4 tbsp) Butter (melted)

2 large eggs

½ cup of Almond Meal

¼ cup of Sugar-Free Raspberry Syrup (or better still desired flavor)

2-8oz. of packages Cream Cheese (softened)

1 teaspoon of Vanilla

Directions:

1. First, you heat your oven to 350F bake.
2. After which you grease or line a cupcake tin (you'll need 12 spots)
3. After that, you mix the melted butter in with the almond meal.
4. Then you press the almond meal mixture into the bottoms of the cupcake tins.
5. In a stand mixer, you add the cream cheese, eggs, stevia, sugar-free syrup, and vanilla to the bowl and mix on medium speed until the mixture is smooth.
6. Once the mixture is smooth, you evenly pour the mix into the cupcake tins, filling almost to the top.
7. At this point, you bake in the oven for about 15-17 minutes.
8. Finally, you let stand for 10 minutes before putting into the fridge for at least 30 minutes.

Delicious Chocolate Brownies

Note: this makes a total of 6 servings of Delicious Chocolate Keto Brownies.

Ingredients:

2 tablespoons of cocoa powder (heaped)

9 packets Truvia

Pinch of salt

3 tablespoons of coconut oil

¼ - ½ cup of almond milk

3 large eggs

¼ cup of coconut flour

1 teaspoon of vanilla extract

6 tablespoons of cream cheese

¼ cup of almond flour

¼ teaspoon of baking soda

Directions:

1. Meanwhile, you heat oven to 375 degrees F
2. After which you combine cream cheese, eggs, coconut oil, almond milk, and vanilla extract in one bowl; Mix well until smooth.
3. After that, you combine cocoa powder, baking soda, truvia, almond flour, coconut flour, and salt in another bowl.
4. Then you slowly add wet ingredients to dry and mix well

5. At this point, you pour batter into cake pan or brownie pan and bake for about 30 minutes (or until a toothpick comes out clean)
6. Finally, you let cool 5 minutes and cut as desired.

White Chocolate Bark with A Twist

Note: this makes a total of 12 servings of White Chocolate Bark.

Ingredients:

½ teaspoon of hemp seed powder

2 ounces of cacao butter

Pinch of salt

1/3 cup of erythritol

1 teaspoon of toasted pumpkin seeds

1 teaspoon of vanilla powder

Directions:

1. First, you measure out the 2oz cacao butter and chop finely.
2. After which you put the cacao butter in the top of a double boiler or in a bowl that can be placed over a pan of boiling water.
3. After that, you mix remaining ingredients into a separate bowl and mix well.
4. Then you turn the burner on and bring water in the pan to a low boil over medium high heat.
5. At this point, you continue cooking just until cacao butter is melted.
6. Then while cacao butter is melting, grease a small bowl or plate with butter or coconut oil. (NOTE: As soon as the cacao butter is melted, remove from heat and mix in remaining ingredients).
7. This is when you stir well and pour into the greased dish.
8. Finally, once the mixture has set, remove from dish and break into 12 equal pieces. (NOTE: To speed up this process, you can place the dish in the freezer for about 15 minutes)

9. Make sure you put them away and enjoy as a great snack!

Pumpkin Snickerdoodle Cookies

Note: this makes a total of 15 Keto Pumpkin Snickerdoodle Cookies.

Ingredients:

The Cookies

1 teaspoon of Vanilla Extract

25 drops of Liquid Stevia

½ cup of Pumpkin Puree

¼ cup of Erythritol

¼ cup of Butter (salted)

1 large Egg

1 ½ cups of Almond Flour

½ teaspoon of Baking Powder

The Topping:

1 teaspoon of Pumpkin Pie Spice

2 teaspoons of Erythritol

Directions:

1. Meanwhile, you heat oven to 350F.
2. After which you measure out dry ingredients and mix.
3. Then in a separate container, you measure out the butter, pumpkin puree, vanilla, and liquid stevia.
4. At this point, you mix everything together well until a pastry dough is formed.

5. After that, you roll the dough into small balls and set on a cookie sheet covered with a Silpat. (NOTE: About 15 cookies in total.)
6. Furthermore, you press the balls flat with your hand (or the bottom side of a jar) and bake for about 12-13 minutes.
7. Finally, while the cookies are cooking, run 2 teaspoons of erythritol and 1 teaspoon of pumpkin pie spice through a spice grinder.
8. Once the cookies are done, I suggest you sprinkle with the topping and let cool completely.

Vanilla Cream Cheese Frosting
Ingredients:

½ teaspoon of vanilla extract

3 tablespoons of heavy whipping cream

¼ cup of powdered erythritol

4 ounces of cream cheese

Directions:

1. Meanwhile, you heat oven to 350° F while gathering your ingredients.
2. After which, in a medium sized bowl, mix the eggs, mayonnaise, and vanilla bean paste.
3. If you want the batter to be really smooth, I suggest you use a hand mixer.
4. After that, you set the bowl to the side.
5. Then in another bowl, mix together the almond flour, erythritol, salt, and baking powder.
6. At this point, you slowly whisk the batter into the almond flour. (NOTE: if you have a hard time mixing them together, I suggest you use the hand blender until it is smooth.)
7. However, the mixture will seem a little dry when it's mixed, but this is normal.
8. Furthermore, using a ¼ cup measure, spoon out eight servings into a lined muffin or cupcake pan.
9. Finally, you bake for 20-25 minutes at 350° F or until they're lightly browned on top.
10. Make sure you frost after they have cooled.

Chai Spice Mug Cake

Ingredients:

Base

1 tablespoon of erythritol

1 large egg

7 drops of liquid Stevia

2 tablespoons of butter

½ teaspoon of baking powder

2 tablespoons of almond flour

Flavor

¼ teaspoon of clove

2 tablespoons of almond flour

¼ teaspoon of cardamom

¼ teaspoon of cinnamon

¼ teaspoon of vanilla extract

¼ teaspoon of ginger

Directions:

1. First, you mix all room temperature ingredients together in a mug.
2. After which you microwave on high for 70 seconds.
3. After that, you turn the cup upside down and lightly bang it against a plate.

4. **Optional:** feel free to top with whipped cream and sprinkle of cinnamon.

Low Carb Cookie Butter

Note: this makes about 1 cup of Low Carb Cookie Butter.

Ingredients:

¼ teaspoon of Cinnamon

2 tablespoons of Butter

1 cup of Raw Macadamias

¼ teaspoon of Ginger

2 tablespoons of Swerve (powdered)

¾ cup of Raw Cashews

1/8 teaspoon of Nutmeg

Pinch Salt

1 teaspoon of Vanilla

1/8 teaspoon of Cloves

2 tablespoons of Heavy Cream

Directions:

1. First, you add macadamia nuts and cashews into food processor and process until smooth.
2. After which you brown the butter with the powdered Swerve in a saucepan.
3. Then once butter is brown, add heavy cream and stir into the butter.
4. After that, you remove from heat.
5. At this point, you add vanilla and spices, then process again until well combined and little to no lumps inside.

NOTE: While processing, pour in caramel sauce and continue the process until you're happy with the consistency.

Coconut Peanut Butter Balls

Ingredients:

½ cup of unsweetened coconut flakes

2 teaspoons of almond flour

3 teaspoons of unsweetened cocoa powder

3 tablespoons of creamy peanut butter

2 ½ teaspoons of powdered erythritol

Directions:

1. First, you mix together your cocoa, peanut butter, erythritol, and flour, in a bowl.
2. After which you freeze for one hour.
3. Using a melon baller (or better still small spoon), spoon out a small serving of the peanut butter mix.
4. After that, you drop it into your coconut flakes and roll around with your hands so the coconut covers the ball. (NOTE: Reshape into a ball if needed.)
5. Finally, you refrigerate overnight so they firm up.

Cream Cheese Truffles

Ingredients:

¼ teaspoon of liquid Stevia

24 paper candy cups (for serving)

4 tablespoons of Swerve confectioners

1 tablespoon of heavy whipping cream

½ cup of unsweetened cocoa powder (divided)

1 tablespoon of instant coffee

16 ounces' cream cheese (softened)

½ teaspoon of rum extract

2 tablespoons of water

Directions:

1. First, in a large bowl add the ¼ cup of cocoa powder, instant coffee, cream cheese, rum extract, Swerve, Stevia, water, and heavy whipping cream.
2. After which you use an electric hand mixer to whip all of the ingredients together until they are well combined.
3. After that, you place the bowl in the fridge for half an hour to chill before rolling.
4. Then you spread the remaining ¼ cup cocoa powder out.
5. At this point, you roll heaping tablespoons in the palm of your hand to form balls, then roll them around in the cocoa powder. (NOTE: You will end up with about 24 totals.)
6. Finally, you place them individually in small paper candy cups.
7. Make sure you chill for an hour before serving.

Delectable Dinner Recipes

Hasselback Marinara Chicken

Note: this makes a total of 6 servings of Hassel back Marinara Chicken.

Ingredients:

3 whole chicken breasts

salt and pepper (to taste)

10 ounce of package frozen spinach (thawed with water squeezed out)

3 ounces of mozzarella slices

1/3 cup of shredded mozzarella

2/3 cup of Rao's homemade (tomato basil sauce)

4 ounces of cream cheese

1 tablespoon of olive oil

Directions:

1. Meanwhile, you heat your oven to 400°F.
2. After which you place the mozzarella, cream cheese, and spinach in a microwave safe bowl.
3. After that, you heat for about 2 minutes, or until the cheeses get melty and can be easily mixed together.
4. Then you mix the filling and add salt and pepper to taste.
5. At this point, you cut several horizontal slices across each chicken breast, cut as deeply as you can without slicing all the way through the chicken.
6. After that, you season the chicken with salt and pepper.
7. This is when you stuff each piece of chicken with the cheese filling.

8. Furthermore, you brush some olive oil onto the bare chicken tops.
9. After which, you cook for 25 minutes, or until chicken reaches 165°F.
10. At this point, you change your oven to the broil setting.
11. Then you top with Rao's tomato sauce, and the slices of mozzarella.
12. Finally, you broil for 5 minutes, or until the cheese gets melty and starts to brown.

Low Carb Sweet and Sour Meatballs

Note: this makes a total of 5 servings of Sweet and Sour Meatballs.

Ingredients:

The meatballs:

½ teaspoon of onion powder

¼ cup of Parmesan cheese

1 large egg

1 pound of ground beef

Ingredients for the sauce:

1/3 cup of sugar-free ketchup

1 ½ cups of water

1 cup of erythritol

¼ cup of apple cider vinegar

½ teaspoon of xanthan gum

3 tablespoons of soy sauce

Directions:

1. First, in a large mixing bowl add an egg, ground beef, grated Parmesan cheese, and onion powder.
2. After which you mix together with your hands.
3. After that, you use a tablespoon to measure, shape the meatballs. (NOTE: You should be able to form 30 mini meatballs.)
4. Meanwhile, you heat a saucepan over medium heat.

5. Then you add the meatballs and cook until browned on the outside. (NOTE: If it's slightly pink in the middle, that's okay for now.); Put to the side.
6. Furthermore, in the same sauce pan add the water, sugar-free ketchup, apple cider vinegar, soy sauce, and erythritol.
7. After that, you use a whisk to stir until the sauce comes together.
8. Furthermore, you slowly whisk in the xanthan gum. (NOTE: stir in a little at a time, waiting a couple minutes in between to make sure it thickens.)
9. After which you lower the temperature, and let the sauce simmer on low.
10. Then after a couple of minutes, check the sauce to make sure it's the desired consistency. Dip a spoon into the sauce to see if it coats the back.
11. Remember, if you run your finger across the back of the spoon, a thickened sauce will not immediately run back together. Careful not to burn yourself.
12. Finally, you add the meatballs, and let them simmer on low for about 10 minutes or until the meatballs are fully cooked through.

Skillet Browned Chicken with Creamy Greens

Ingredients:

1 cup of cream

Salt and pepper (to taste)

1 cup of chicken stock

2 Tablespoons of coconut flour

2 Tablespoons of coconut oil

2 cups of dark leafy greens

1 lb. of chicken thighs (boneless but skin on)

1 teaspoon of Italian herbs

2 Tablespoons of butter (melted)

Directions:

1. Meanwhile, you heat a large skillet on a medium-high setting.
2. After which you add two tablespoons of coconut oil to the pan.
3. After that, you season both sides of the chicken thighs with salt and pepper while the oil heats up.
4. Then brown chicken thighs in the skillet.
5. At this point, you fry both sides until the chicken is cooked through and crispy.
6. Then, while the thighs are cooking you should start the sauce.
7. If you want to create the sauce, first, you melt two tablespoons of butter in a sauce pan.
8. Furthermore, once the butter stops sizzling, whisk in two tablespoons of coconut flour to form a thick paste.
9. After which you whisk in one cup of cream and bring the mixture to a boil. (NOTE: The mixture should thicken after a few minutes.
10. After that, you stir in the teaspoon of Italian herbs.

11. This is when you remove cooked chicken thighs from the skillet and set aside.
12. Then you pour the cup of chicken stock into the chicken skillet and deglaze the pan.
13. Whisk in the cream sauce and stir the greens into the pan so that they become coated with the sauce.
14. Finally, you lay the chicken thighs back on top of the greens, then remove from the heat and serve.
15. Divide chicken and greens up into four servings size.

Spicy Sausage & Cabbage Skillet Melt

Ingredients:

½ cup of diced onion

4 spicy Italian chicken sausages

2 slices (about 1 ounce each) of Colby Jack cheese

1 ½ cups of green cabbage (shredded)

2 Tablespoons of chopped fresh cilantro

1 ½ cups of purple cabbage (shredded)

2 Tablespoons of coconut oil

Directions:

1. First, you remove casings from sausages and rough chop.
2. After which you chop the onion and shred cabbage (if you not using pre-shredded cabbage.)
3. After that, you melt coconut oil in a large skillet and add onion and cabbage.
4. Then you cook over medium-high heat until the vegetables begin to become tender, about 8 minutes.
5. This is when you add sausage, stirring to mix it into the cabbage and onions.
6. Furthermore, you cook 8 minutes more.
7. After which you add the cheese on top and cover the skillet.
8. Then you turn off the heat and wait 5 minutes while the cheese melts into the cabbage and vegetables.
9. After that, you remove the lid from the skillet and stir.
10. Finally, you top with cilantro and serve immediately right from the skillet.

Reverse Seared Ribeye Steak

Note: this makes a total of 3 servings of Reverse Seared Ribeye Steak.

Ingredients:

Salt and Pepper (to Taste)

3 tablespoons of Bacon Fat (or better still other high smoke point oil)

2 medium Ribeye Steaks (about 1.2 lbs.)

Directions:

1. Meanwhile, heat oven to 250F.
2. After which you put your steaks on a wire rack on top of a cookie sheet.
3. After that, season heavily with salt and pepper on all sides.
4. Then you stick an instant-read thermometer through the side of the steak.
5. At this point, you bake in the oven until internal temperature of 123F is reached.
6. After that, you heat the bacon grease in a cast iron skillet and wait until the pan is very hot.
7. Finally, you place the steaks in and sear for 30 - 45 seconds on each side.

Chicken Zoodles

Note: this makes 1 serving of Thai Chicken Zoodles.

Ingredients:

1 tablespoon of Coconut Oil

1.4 oz. of Bean Sprouts

1/8 teaspoon of White Pepper

½ teaspoon of Curry Powder

1 stalk of Spring Onion

3.5 oz. of Zucchini

Red Chilies (chopped)

3.5 oz. of Chicken Thigh

1 clove of Garlic

1 teaspoon of Soy Sauce (or better still Coconut Amino)

Pinch of Salt and Pepper

1 tablespoon of Unsalted Butter

1 large Egg

½ teaspoon of Oyster Sauce

1 teaspoon of Lime Juice

Directions:

1. First, you marinate Chicken with Curry Powder and Salt and Pepper.
2. After which, you prepare the sauce by combining Oyster Sauce, Soy Sauce, and White Pepper.

3. After that, you chop finely the Spring Onion and Garlic and make Zoodles out of Zucchini.
4. At this point, you fry the Chicken with Unsalted Butter until brown; sliced to bite-sized pieces.
5. Then, with the same pan on high heat, add Coconut oil.
6. Furthermore, you sauté chopped Spring Onion until fragrant.
7. Add in chopped Garlic.
8. This is when you crack an Egg and scramble.
9. After that, you brown the egg slightly.
10. Then you add Bean Sprouts and Zoodles and mix in the sauce.
11. Make sure you thicken the sauce a bit.
12. Add in fried Chicken pieces and stir.
13. Finally, you garnish with chopped Red Chilies and squeeze Lime Juice.
14. Serve!

Cheddar Bacon Explosion
Ingredients:

2 teaspoons of Mrs. Dash Table Seasoning

1-2 Tablespoons of Tones Southwest Chipotle Seasoning

2 ½ Cups of Cheddar Cheese

30 Slices of Bacon

4-5 Cups of Raw Spinach

Directions:

1. Meanwhile, you heat your oven to 375F convection bake.
2. After which, weave the bacon. 15 pieces that are vertical, 12 pieces' horizontal, and the extra 3 cut in half to fill in rest, horizontally.
3. After that, you season your bacon with your favorite seasoning mix.
4. Then you add your cheese to the bacon, leaving about 1 ½ inch gaps between the edges.
5. Furthermore, add your spinach and press down on it to compress it some. (NOTE: this will help when you roll it up.)
6. After which you roll your weave slowly, making sure it stays tight and not too much falls through.
7. Remember, you may have some cheese fall out, but don't worry about it.
8. After that, you add your seasoning to the outside here.
9. Then you foil a baking sheet and add plenty of salt to it. (NOTE: this will help catch excess grease from the bacon and not let your oven smoke.)
10. At this point, you put your bacon on top of a cooling rack and put that on top of your baking sheet.

11. This is when you bake for about 60-70 minutes, without opening the oven door. (NOTE: pour bacon should be very crisp on the top when finished.)
12. Finally, you let cool for 10-15 minutes before trying to take it off the cooling rack.

Make sure you slice into pieces and serve!

General Tso's Chicken

Ingredients:

Chicken

2 Large Eggs

6-7 Small Chicken Breasts

2 Tablespoons of Olive Oil

¾ Cup of Crushed Pork Rinds

1 Tablespoon of Coconut Oil

1/3 Cup of Almond Flour

Sauce

2 Tablespoons of Reduced Sugar Ketchup

1 teaspoon of Red Chili Paste

¼ teaspoon of Xanthan Gum

2 ½ Tablespoons of Soy Sauce

1 teaspoon of Hoisin Sauce

½ teaspoon of Minced Ginger

3 Tablespoons of Rice Vinegar

2 teaspoons of Sesame Oil

1 teaspoon of Garlic Powder

¼ Cup of Chicken Broth

2 Tablespoons of Erythritol

1 teaspoon of Red Chili Flakes

Optional:

NOTE: garnish with chives, red chili pepper flakes, or red chili peppers.

Directions:

1. First, you put pork rinds in the food processor and pulse them until crushed.
2. After which you combine almond flour with pork rinds in one bowl, scramble 2 eggs in another bowl.
3. Meanwhile, you heat oven to 325F.
4. After that, you wash and cube chicken breasts.
5. Then you dip chicken in egg, dip chicken in pork rinds and almond flour.
6. Furthermore, you fry chicken in olive and coconut oil.
7. This is when you make the sauce and cover chicken with sauce.
8. Finally, you bake chicken in sauce for 1 hour, turning/mixing chicken every 15 minutes.

Creamy Spinach Pork Tenderloin Roulade

Note: this makes 4 servings in total.

Ingredients:

5 slices of Prosciutto

Salt and Pepper (to taste)

2 teaspoons + 1 teaspoons of Minced Garlic

¼ teaspoon of Mrs. Dash Table Blend

3 tablespoons + 1 teaspoons of Olive Oil

4 oz. of Cream Cheese

1 lb. of Pork Tenderloin

6-7 cups of Spinach

Directions:

1. Meanwhile, you heat oven to 450F.
2. After which, you bitterly the pork tenderloin by cutting 1 or 2 strips through the meat of the pork.
3. After that, you put plastic wrap over pork and pound out the meat to ½ inch thickness using the smooth side of the meat hammer.
4. Then you season with salt and pepper and pound lightly with the spiked side of meat hammer.
5. At this point, you add olive oil to the pan can bring to high heat.
6. This is when you add garlic and let cook for about 30-60 seconds, then add spinach and sauté until wilted.
7. Furthermore, you lay slices of prosciutto over pork tenderloin to cover the entire surface.
8. Pour spinach over the pork tenderloin. (NOTE: make sure all the oil gets in there too.)

9. After that, you rip pieces of cream cheese off and lay them on the pork.
10. After which you roll the pork up and use toothpicks to secure the end. Feel free to use butchers string to do this.
11. Then you add seasonings to outside of pork (preferably, pepper, Mrs. Dash, and minced garlic).
12. Finally, you bake for about 20 minutes at 450F and then reduce heat to 325F and cook for 60-75 minutes until internal temperature reads 145F.

Paprika Chicken

Note: this makes 4 total servings.

Ingredients:

2 Tablespoons of Lemon Juice (1 Lemon)

4 Boneless, Skinless Chicken Breasts

2 teaspoons of Minced Garlic

3 Tablespoons of Olive Oil

Salt and Pepper

2 Tablespoons of Spanish Smoked Paprika

1 Tablespoons of Maple Syrup

Directions:

1. Meanwhile, you heat oven to 350F.
2. After which you prep chicken by cutting into chunks and seasoning with salt and pepper.
3. After that, you prep sauce by combining all other ingredients.
4. Then you add 1/3 of sauce to the bottom of a casserole dish and lay chicken on top of it.
5. At this point, you spread to rest of sauce thoroughly over all pieces of chicken, then put in the oven for 30-35 minutes.
6. Finally, to finish the chicken off, broil for an additional 4-5 minutes.

Low Carb Chicken Satay

Yields 3 servings.

Ingredients:

2 Spring of Onions

2 teaspoons of Sesame Oil

Juice of ½ Lime

3 Tablespoons of Peanut Butter

1 Tablespoon of Rice Vinegar

¼ teaspoon of Paprika

4 Tablespoons of Soy Sauce

1 Tablespoon of Erythritol

1 teaspoon of Minced Garlic

1 lb. of Ground Chicken

1/3 Yellow Pepper

2 teaspoons of Chili Paste

¼ teaspoon of Cayenne

Directions:

1. First, you heat 2 teaspoons of sesame oil on medium-high heat in a pan.
2. After which brown ground chicken, then add all other ingredients.
3. After that, you mix well and continue cooking.
4. Then once everything is cooked, add 2 chopped spring onions and 1/3 sliced yellow pepper.

Baked Sea Bass with Herb Cauliflower Salad

Note: this makes a total of 2 servings of Baked Sea Bass with Herbed Cauliflower Salad.

Ingredients:

3 tablespoons of extra virgin olive oil

Salt and pepper (to taste)

10 ounces' whole sea bass (cleaned and scaled)

2 small lemon

1/3 cup of fresh mint

1/3 cup of green olives

1/3 cup of flat leaf parsley

1 cup of finely grated cauliflower

Directions:

1. Meanwhile, you heat the oven to 400°F.
2. After which you finely chop the parsley and mint.
3. After that, you prepare the sea bass by placing on baking parchment in a baking dish and rub with 1 tablespoon extra-virgin olive oil.
4. This you season with salt and pepper.
5. At this point, you thinly slice one of the lemons then stuff into the sea bass with a small amount of the fresh herbs.
6. After which you bake in the oven for 15 minutes, or until the thickest part of the fish is cooked.
7. In the meantime, finely chop the olives. Zest and juice the other lemon.
8. Furthermore, in a large bowl mix together the grated cauliflower, lemon zest, herbs, olives, lemon juice and 2 tablespoons of extra virgin olive oil.

9. After that, you season with salt and pepper to taste.
10. Finally, you remove the sea bass from the oven when cooked and serve with the herbed cauliflower salad.

Spicy Cauliflower Rice & Salmon Medley

Note: this makes a total of 6 servings of Spicy Cauliflower Rice & Salmon Medley.

Ingredients:

1 medium (about 119 g) orange bell pepper (chopped)

2 tablespoons of Japanese 7-spice (shichimi togarashi)

2 tablespoons of olive oil

2 tablespoons of (20 g) shallot (finely diced)

1 medium (588 g) cauliflower (diced)

4 (about 4-oz) fillets salmon (cubed into 2-inch pieces)

4 tablespoons of soy sauce

Salt and pepper (to taste)

1 small (50 g) carrot (chopped)

2 tablespoons of sesame oil

Directions:

1. First, in a medium sized stock-pot, preheat your olive oil on medium heat.
2. After which you sauté the salmon cubes for about 5 minutes, stirring occasionally until they have gone from pink to white.
3. After that, you add in the carrot, peppers, and shallots.
4. Then you sauté for 5 minutes.
5. At this point, you stir in the soy sauce and sesame oil, making sure you coat all the vegetables and fish.

6. Furthermore, you season the veggies with the 7-spice powder then stir and let the fish soak up the soy and sesame for 2-3 minutes.
7. After that, you add the cauliflower rice and mix in with a wooden spoon.
8. Then you turn your stove up to medium-high to fry the cauliflower; stir occasionally.
9. Finally, you taste! Use a little more spice if needed, then season with salt and pepper.

Low Carb Sweet and Sour Meatballs

Note: this makes a total of 5 servings of Sweet and Sour Meatballs.

Ingredients:

The meatballs:

½ teaspoon of onion powder

¼ cup of Parmesan cheese

1 large egg

1 pound of ground beef

Ingredients for the sauce:

1/3 cup of sugar-free ketchup

1 ½ cups of water

1 cup of erythritol

¼ cup of apple cider vinegar

½ teaspoon of xanthan gum

3 tablespoons of soy sauce

Directions:

1. First, in a large mixing bowl add ground beef, an egg, grated Parmesan cheese, and onion powder.
2. After which you mix together with your hands.
3. After that, you use a tablespoon to measure, shape the meatballs. (NOTE: You should be able to form 30 mini meatballs.)
4. Meanwhile, you heat a saucepan over medium heat.

5. Then you add the meatballs and cook until browned on the outside. (NOTE: If it's slightly pink in the middle, that's okay for now.); put to the side.
6. Furthermore, in the same sauce pan add the water, soy sauce, apple cider vinegar, sugar-free ketchup, and erythritol.
7. After which you use a whisk to stir until the sauce comes together.
8. After that, you slowly whisk in the xanthan gum. (NOTE: stir in a little at a time, waiting a couple minutes in between to make sure it thickens.)
9. At this point, you lower the temperature, and let the sauce simmer on low.
10. Then after a couple of minutes, check the sauce to make sure it's the desired consistency. (NOTE: feel free to dip a spoon into the sauce to see if it coats the back.)
11. Remember, if you run your finger across the back of the spoon, a thickened sauce will not immediately run back together. Careful not to burn yourself.
12. Finally, you add the meatballs and let them simmer on low for 10 minutes or until the meatballs are fully cooked through.

Blackberry Chipotle Chicken Wings

Note: this makes a total of 20 Blackberry Chipotle Chicken Wings.

Ingredients:

Salt and Pepper (to Taste)

½ cup of Water

½ cup of Blackberry Chipotle Jam

3 lbs. of Chicken Wings (about 20 wings, butchered)

Directions:

1. First, you butcher the chicken wings by separating drum mettes, wings, and wing tips.
2. After which you freeze wing tips for use in bone broth.
3. After that, you combine Blackberry Chipotle Jam and water in a bowl.
4. This is when you whisk to combine, then add 2/3 marinade with the chicken wings in a plastic bag.
5. At this point, you season with salt and pepper to taste.
6. Furthermore, you let this sit for at least 30 minutes, or overnight.
7. Then, once ready, preheat oven to 400F.
8. This is when you lay chicken on a cookie sheet with a wire rack on top.
9. After that, you bake for 15 minutes at 400F, then flip and turn the oven up to 425F.
10. Finally, you brush the remaining marinade over each wing (now the bottom side) and bake for 20-30 minutes.

Hearty Crock Pot Chicken Stew

Note: this makes about 5 big servings,

Ingredients:

1 ½ Cup of Tomato Sauce (I prefer Classico Tomato and Basil)

2 teaspoons of Ranch Seasoning

1 teaspoon of Oregano

3 Cups of Mushrooms

3 Tablespoons of Butter

1 teaspoon of Red Pepper Flakes

1 Medium Green Pepper

1/3 Cup of Hot Wing Sauce

2 teaspoons of Paprika

3 lbs. of Chicken Thigh

½ Cup of Sliced Tomatoes

2 teaspoons of Minced Garlic

Directions:

1. First, you chop mushrooms and pepper into thin slices.
2. After which you turn crock pot to high heat.
3. After that, you add chicken thighs, garlic, tomato sauce, slide tomato, spices, and hot sauce to crock pot.
4. Then you add peppers and onions to chicken mixture, mix thoroughly.
5. This is when you let simmer on high for 2 hours.
6. At this point, you turn crock pot to low, stir ingredients.
7. After that, you allow cooking for another 3-5 hours.

8. Then you add 3 tablespoons of butter to your stew and stir together. (Optional: ½ teaspoon of xanthan gum for thickening.)
9. Finally, you cook for another hour without the lid so the sauce can reduce.
10. You can serve hot and enjoy or better still store it in the fridge and reheat for meals later in the microwave.

Delectable Sides and salad

Sundried Tomato Tuna Salad

Things you will need: *small bowl, fork, cutting board and knife*
Yield: 1-2 servings

Ingredients:

4-5 sundried tomatoes (chopped up)
1 can of Albacore tuna (packed in water)
Baked Sweet Potato Discs (recipe follows)
1 avocado
Sliced cucumber
Salt and pepper (to taste)
¼ cup of fresh parsley (chopped fine)

Directions:

1. First, in a small bowl, mash avocado and tuna together.
2. After which you chop sundried tomato and parsley, and mix it in.
3. After that, you add salt and pepper.
4. Then you serve on baked sweet potato discs and/or cucumber slices.

Tuna Avocado Salad

Yield: 1 serving
things you will need: *mesh strainer, fork, knife, can opener, mixing bowl, cutting board, measuring spoons*

Tip:

Remember that these delightful little bite-sized snacks can be made with 3 simples

Ingredients:
2 Tablespoons of spicy mustard
1 can tuna
½ avocado

Directions:

1. First, you mash everything together.
2. However, you can serve them on sliced cucumbers with a little slivered carrot and cilantro garnish (as shown), or add diced shallots to spice them up a little more.

Note: I have also added chopped celery, parsley and some crushed ground pepper to make another variation.

Chia Seed Strawberry Jam

Yield: 3 servings

Things you will need: *food processor or blender, small pot, wooden spoon, measuring spoon*

Ingredients:

2-4 Tablespoons of coconut sugar (or better still honey, agave, another natural sweetener, or none!)

1 Tablespoon of chia seeds

About 10-12 fresh, organic strawberries

Directions:

1. First, you cut off the tops of your strawberries and blend them until evenly shredded.
2. After which you transfer them to a small pot, and add the chia seeds.
3. After that, you cook the strawberries and chia seed mixture on the stovetop on medium-high heat, stirring constantly for about 10 minutes.
4. Then once the mixture has begun to thicken and get sticky – it will darken slightly in color as well.
5. This is when you reduce heat and add the sugar.
6. Furthermore, you stir together for a couple more minutes, and remove from heat.
7. At this point, it will be sticky and jam-like, and after you chill it even more so.

Notes

I have made the same recipe using blueberries and raspberries as well – and to fruits that are less juicy than strawberries I advise adding a tablespoon or two of water with the mashed berries before you start so the chia seeds can absorb more liquid, and become even more gel-like.

Bacon Cauliflower Mash

Yield: 4 servings

things you will need: *large Dutch oven, skillet, knife, cutting board, spatula, food processor, measuring cups and spoons*

Ingredients:

½ cup of almond milk (more or less depending on how thick you want it)

1 head purple (or better still regular) cauliflower

1 onion (chopped)

1 Tablespoon of walnut (or better still olive) oil

2 slices of turkey bacon (make sure you look for uncured turkey bacon with the least sodium and at least 12g of protein per 2 slices)
2 cloves garlic (minced)

Directions:

1. First, you wash and prep your cauliflower, and boil it for 5-8 min or until a fork pierced it easily.
2. After which you pan sear the bacon.
3. After that, once your bacon is done you can cut it into strips.
4. Then you sauté the onion and garlic until the onion is translucent (I prefer walnut oil because it's amazing).
5. At this point, you add the cauliflower to your food processor and blend it with a little almond milk.
6. Finally, you add the onion/garlic and bacon and blend away.

NOTE: I served this recipe with some of that herbed turkey breast recipe I shared with you guys a while back and some fresh organic tomatoes. Amazing!!!

Brussels Sprout Cherry Tomato Salad

Yield: 1 serving
things you will need: *knife, cutting board, mixing bowl, skillet, mixing spoon, measuring cups and spoons*

Ingredients:

2 teaspoons of (approximately) Balsamic vinegar

1 Tablespoon of walnut oil

½ cup of cherry tomatoes

½ lb. of Brussel sprouts

Directions:

1. First, you wash and trim brussels sprouts
2. After which you Sautee sprouts in walnut oil in a skillet over medium heat for approximately 10 minutes.
3. After that, you halve cherry tomatoes and set aside.
4. Then you add a splash of balsamic vinegar, and cook for 1 minute longer.
5. Finally, you toss sprouts in a bowl with halved cherry tomatoes.

Tuna Salad on Sliced Cucumbers

Yield: 1 serving

things you will need: *can opener, mesh strainer, fork, knife, cutting board, mixing bowl*

Ingredients:

Fresh ground pepper

2 Tablespoons of spicy mustard

Assorted veggies you have on hand (tomatoes, celery, shallots)

½ ripe avocado

1-5oz can albacore tuna, packed in water, with no salt added

Directions:

1. First, you mix everything in a bowl.
2. Then you slice ½ a cucumber and spread tuna salad on top.

Sesame Zucchini Cucumber Salad

Yield: 2 servings
things you will need: *knife, cutting board, measuring spoon, medium sized mixing bowl*

Ingredients:

1-2 shallots

1 cucumber

3 Tablespoons of parsley

1 lemon (juice of)

2 Tablespoons of sesame seeds

1 zucchini

2 Tablespoons of sesame oil
Fresh ground pepper

Directions:

1. First, you slice zucchini and cucumber in thin strips, working your way around until you're down to the seeds (**NOTE:** you can choose to include the center with the seeds or not).

2. After which you add the strips to a medium size mixing bowl.

3. After that, you rough chop parsley, and dice shallots.

4. Then you add to the zucchini.

5. At this point, you add these sesame oil, lemon and sesame seeds.

6. Finally, you mix all ingredients together, and add a little fresh ground pepper to taste.

Delectable Dip and Spread Recipes

Paleo Macadamia Nut Pesto Rolls
Yield: 1 serving
things you will need: *food processor, cutting board, and knife*

Ingredients:

1 ½ cups of fresh basil (feel free to add spinach to stretch it out if you're short on basil)

3 Tablespoons of macadamia nuts
2-3 Tablespoons of olive oil

3-4 cloves garlic (with skin removed)

Directions:

1. First, you wash and pat basil leaves dry.
2. After which you place them in the food processor and pulse until evenly chopped.
3. After that, you add macadamia nuts and garlic and blend until smooth.
4. However, you may want to stop and scrape the sides down once or twice to ensure an even chop.
5. At this point, you add olive oil and blend (NOTE: You may add more or less olive oil, depending on your desired consistency).

Directions on how to assemble Omelets Roll

1. *First, in* a small bowl, whisk 2 eggs together until foamy.
2. After which you heat a medium sized skillet and coat with coconut oil.
3. After that, you pour in eggs and cook until nearly cooked through.
4. Then you flip and finish briefly on the sunny side.

5. At this point, you transfer your omelet to a plate and spread with 2 Tablespoons of pesto.
6. Finally, you roll up and garnish with tomatoes and sea salt.

Raw Creamy Avocado Pesto

Yield: about 1/2 cup

things you will need: *food processor, cutting board, knife, liquid measuring cup, measuring cups and spoons*

Ingredients:

3 Tablespoons of hemp seeds

1 cup of fresh basil

2 cloves garlic

1 avocado (ripe)

¼ cup of olive oil (for a more sauce like consistency, add 3-4 Tablespoons of water)

½ cup of walnuts

DIRECTIONS:

1. First, you de-seed your avocado, and scoop it out of its skin into the food processor.
2. After which you remove the skin from the garlic and add it to the food processor.
3. Then you add all the remaining ingredients and blend until creamy.
4. Because the avocado will oxidize quickly and turn your pesto brown, I suggest you squeeze some fresh lemon in to keep it fresh looking longer.
5. **NOTE:** when you take it out after storing, I suggest you just give it a quick stir and its paler green will be revealed.

Parsley-Thyme Spinach Pesto

Yield: 1 cup Prep time: 10 minutes
things you will need: *food processor, spatula, measuring cups and spoons*

Ingredients:

¼ cup of walnuts

fresh black pepper (to taste)

1 Teaspoon of thyme, de-stemmed

¼ teaspoons of salt

1 cup of parsley, de-stemmed

½ lemon (juice and zest)

1 cup of spinach (packed)

4 garlic cloves

¼ cup of olive oil

Directions:

1. First, you remove the parsley from its stems.
2. After which you measure it by packing it tightly into a cup.
3. After that, you pack the spinach tightly to measure as well and add both to the food processor.
4. At this point you pluck the leaves of thyme from its stems and add them along with the greens.
5. This is when you pulse the greens together until they've formed a fine, even consistency. I prefer to use pulse to help the leaves settle, and occasionally open the top to scrape down the sides with a spatula.
6. Then you peel the garlic and add it, along with the walnuts.

7. Furthermore, you blend until sticky.
8. After which you remove the lid of the food processor and grate or zest half a lemon.
9. After that, you squeeze its juice in.
10. Finally, you run the processor again, and slowly add the olive oil. You may want to add a little more or a little less, depending on how you like your consistency.
11. Then you scrape the pesto into a bowl or container and add the salt and pepper.

Healthy Chicken Nuggets

Yield: 2 servings
things you will need: *measuring spoons and cups, meat cutting board, sharp knife, 2 bowls, baking sheet, parchment paper*

Ingredients:

½ cup of unsweetened coconut flakes

salt and pepper to taste

½ cup of almond meal flour

½ teaspoon of onion powder

1 egg

8 oz boneless, skinless chicken breast

½ teaspoon of garlic powder

Directions:

1. Meanwhile, you heat oven to 350.
2. After which you line a baking sheet with parchment paper and set aside.
3. After that, you prepare chicken by cutting it into even sized pieces.
4. Then you set out 2 bowls.
5. In the first bowl, I beat egg, while in the second bowl, you combine almond meal flour, coconut flakes and spices.
6. Furthermore, you dip chicken into egg, then into batter to coat.
7. Make sure you've gotten the entire piece of chicken covered.
8. At this point, you lay it on the baking sheet.
9. Finally, this is when you coat all chicken and bake for about 20-25 minutes, or until batter begins to brown slightly on the outside and the chicken is cooked through.

Cream of Broccoli Soup" (dairy free)

Yield: 4 servings
things you will need: *blender, wide saucepan, knife, cutting board, measuring cup*

Ingredients:

salt and pepper to taste

2 cloves garlic
1-2 cups of water (enough to cover broccoli in pan)

½ cup of hemp seeds

1 head broccoli

Directions:

1. First, you wash and cut broccoli into even sized pieces and place into a saucepan or skillet.

2. After which you add just enough water to cover the broccoli, and place on stovetop.

3. After that, you bring to a boil and cook broccoli until a fork pierces your pieces and they are cooked through, about 5-8 minutes.

4. Then you add broccoli and water to your high-speed blender (or food processor).

5. At this point, you add garlic, hemp seeds and salt and pepper and blend (**NOTE:** After you have blended you may want to

taste and check the consistency, possibly adding more water to smooth it out like I did).

6. Furthermore, once you've achieved the desired consistency and flavor, I suggest you pour a serving into a bowl and add chicken nuggets.

7. Finally, you garnish with fresh parsley or a little fresh pepper.

8. Enjoy!

Tips:

I suggest you store your chicken nuggets and broccoli soup in separate containers so the nuggets don't get soggy.

Sun-dried Tomato Spread

Things you will need: *food processor, Sautee pan, spatula or wooden spoon, cutting board and knife, can opener, measuring spoons*

Ingredients:

1 (about 15 oz) can cannellini beans (any white bean is fine)

2 teaspoons of red wine vinegar

¼ cup of sun-dried tomatoes (dry, not packed in oil)

1 clove of garlic

1 teaspoon of dried oregano

1 cup of warm water

2 Tablespoons of olive oil

1/2-1 teaspoon of sea salt

¼ -1/2 cup of chopped onion

1 Tablespoon of lemon juice

1 teaspoon of dried basil

Directions:

1. First, you put the sun-dried tomatoes in a small bowl and cover them with the warm water for 15 minutes.
2. Then while the tomatoes soak, cook the onions in a small pan with a little olive oil until they are brown.
3. After that, you take the tomatoes out of the water and chop them (save the water).

4. At this point, you chop up the garlic into little pieces.
5. This is when you put the beans, sun-dried tomatoes, onions and 2 Tablespoons of water from the tomatoes in a food processor and process until fine.
6. Furthermore, you add the rest of the ingredients and blend until it looks creamy.
7. Finally, you add more of the tomato water if it looks too dry.

Toppings:

Baby spinach

Thinly sliced onion

Sun-dried tomatoes, chopped

Shredded pre-baked chicken

Pesto Shrimp and Quinoa Stack

Yield: 1 serving
things you will need: *measuring cups and spoons, knife, cutting board, small pot, mixing bowl and spoon*

Ingredients:

Fresh parsley or better still Basil

1-2 slices of Tomato

12 peeled shrimp (fresh or frozen)

½ cup of pre-cooked quinoa

2 Tablespoons of BASIL PESTO

Directions:

1. First, you bring a small pot of water to a boil.
2. After which you add shrimp and steam for about 5-6 minutes.
3. After that, you use a 1/2 cup measuring cup, ramekin or other small dish or bowl, pack quinoa tightly into it and turn onto the center of your plate.
4. At this point, you top with a thick slice of tomato.
5. This is when you drain shrimp, remove tails if they have them, and toss in pesto.
6. **NOTE;** The pesto will make the shrimp sticky. I Suggest you use your hands, form the shrimp into a ball and place atop the tomato.
7. Finally, you top with fresh herbs.

Coconut Curry Fettucine with Capello's Gluten-free Pasta

Yield: 4 servings

things you will need: *knife, cutting board, measuring cups and spoons, skillet, wooden spoon, can opener, large pot*

Ingredients:

1 can coconut milk (light or full-fat)
3 cardamom pods, crushed – or better still 1/4 teaspoon of cardamom
1 package Capello's Fettuccine

1 Tablespoon of coconut oil

1-2 teaspoon of fresh ginger (grated)

Salt and pepper (to taste)

3-4 garlic cloves (minced)

1 Tablespoon of curry powder

1 lb. chicken or better still turkey, cubed small

1 onion (chopped)

½ cup of chicken stock (low sodium)

½ cup fresh basil (chopped)

Directions:

1. First, you heat a large skillet to medium and add coconut oil.
2. After which you sauté onions and garlic for 5 -7 minutes.
3. After that, you add curry powder, ginger, cardamom, salt and pepper and stir well.
4. Then you add chicken and cook for about 5 minutes, or until cooked through.

5. At this point, you remove chicken pieces and set aside.
6. Furthermore, you add coconut milk and chicken stock, and reduce over medium heat for about 10 minutes or so.
7. This is when you add chicken back in and add basil.
8. After that, you simmer for a few more minutes.
9. Finally, you remove from heat and serve over Pasta.

Directions for the Pasta

1. First, to time it with your Chicken, place a pot of water to boil on the stove top around step 6 above.
2. Then once you've added your chicken and basil back into the coconut milk and veggies, add Pasta noodles to pot of boiling water, and cook for about 45 seconds.
3. Finally, you rinse and drain.

Notes

Remember, that I would also add tomatoes or peppers to make this dish more colorful, but I don't cook with either of those vegetables too often, as I am easily irritated by plants from the nightshade family. They would make a wonderful addition to this dish.

Easy Garlic Baked Cod with Vegetable Medley

Yield: 2 servings

things you will need: *aluminum foil, cookie sheet, grater, cutting board, knife*

Ingredients:

¼ cup of fresh parsley

Walnut oil (other oil like coconut oil or better still olive oil is great too)

2-3 garlic cloves

Salt and pepper (to taste)

3-4 baby carrots

Fresh lemon slices

2 servings cod (As for me 1/3 lb. is a serving – this piece is about 2/3 lb.)

½ cup of fresh cherry tomatoes

Directions:

1. Meanwhile, you heat oven to 350.
2. After which you line a cookie sheet with a piece of aluminum foil, and place fish on top.
3. After that, you drizzle with oil, and sprinkle a little salt and pepper over the top.
4. At this point, you grate garlic and carrots onto the fish.
5. This is when you add parsley and lemon slices.
6. Top with tomatoes and wrap fish in foil and bake for about 20 minutes.

7. Make sure you serve immediately, or store for up to a day (NOTE: I added some red quinoa when I made this for the lovely Jaxx, who recently featured some of Austin's coolest things on her very cool blog.)

Coconut-Seared Sea Scallops with Raw Kale, Avocado and Salsa

Yield: 2 servings

things you'll need: *cutting board, knife, Sautee pan, tongs or spatula*

Ingredients:

coconut oil

¼ white onion

5-10 stalks kale (washed, de-stemmed and shredded)

1/2 fresh lemon

1 Tablespoon of cilantro

1 avocado (sliced in half, then sliced thin)

¼ cup of fresh salsa:

¼ fresh lime

4-8 U-10 sea scallops

1 small tomato

Directions:

1. First, you dice tomato and onion.
2. After which you combine in a small bowl with finely chopped cilantro.
3. After that, you squeeze lime over top and mix together.
4. Then you add a little fresh ground pepper and sea salt if desired.
5. At this point, heat skillet to medium heat and add coconut oil.
6. Furthermore, you evenly sea scallops on both sides.
7. After that, you prep kale and use it as the base of your plates.

8. This is when you divide avocado on each plate.
9. Finally, you place scallops over greens and top with salsa.
10. Then you squeeze a quarter of a lemon over the greens and serve.

Mustard Dill Crusted Fish Filets

Yield: 2 servings
things you will need: *spatula, baking sheet, measuring cups*

Ingredients:

1/3 cup of citrus/lime gluten- free bread crumbs

2 Tablespoons of stoneground mustard

¼ cup of dill mustard

Two filets of frozen fish of your choice

Directions:

1. First, you spread on filets.
2. After which you sprinkled with about 1/3 cup fresh chopped parsley.
3. Than you bake for about 15 min at 350.

Note:

However, I had some leftover veggies in the refrigerator from my power prep session on Sunday so I didn't have to do anything else, just plated up some sweet potato, broccoli and sliced up about ½ an avocado.

Marinated Buffalo NY Strip Steak

Yield: 3-4 servings
things you will need: *knife, cutting board, measuring cups and spoons, shallow dish, skillet*

Ingredients:

Fresh ground pepper and sea salt

2-3 Tablespoons of balsamic (I prefer the fig-infused balsamic)

1/3 cup of fresh parsley (chopped fine)

1 lb. of buffalo NY Strip steak

Directions:

1. First, you cut up steak into small 1" pieces.
2. After which you place in a shallow dish with parsley, balsamic and a sprinkle of fresh cracked pepper and salt.
3. After that, you allow it to sit for a minimum of 30 min, or up to 4 hours.
   (**NOTE:** You can do this step first and assemble the fig puree, mushroom caps and other toppings in the meantime if you're making it all at once).
4. Then you heat a skillet to medium and add some cooking oil.
5. Finally, you pan sear the steaks evenly on both sides – mine were very thin and took about 2-3 min a side.

Balsamic Fig Puree

Yield: 3-4 servings
things you will need: *blender, measuring spoons*

Ingredients:

Fresh cracked pepper to taste

1 ½ Tablespoons of coconut sugar

1 Tablespoons of balsamic (I prefer a fig infused one)

8-9 fresh figs (washed and de-stemmed)

¼ fresh lemon (juice of)

Directions:

First, you blend all ingredients in a food processor until an even consistency is formed.

Steak Salad

Yield: 2 servings
things you will need: *sharp knives, cutting board, Sautee pan or grill, tongs*

Ingredients:

fresh basil

2 flank steaks (about 1/3- 1/2 lb. each)

2 vine-ripened tomatoes

Salt and pepper

1 avocado

2 cups of baby spinach

Directions:

1. First, you season the steaks with salt and pepper.
2. After which you heat up your grill or skillet, and cook until desired doneness.
3. Then while the steaks are cooking, prepare your salad by filling two bowls with the salad ingredients.
4. After that, you add 1 cup of spinach to each, some fresh basil, 1 sliced tomato to each, and divide the avocado between them.
5. Finally, you slice the steak pieces over the salad and serve with a little fresh ground pepper.

Baked Salmon with Grainy Mustard, Parsley and Sliced Shallots

Yield: 2 servings
things you will need: *A baking sheet, olive oil or coconut oil (spray or regular), knife and cutting board*

Ingredients:

Fresh lemon

1/3 cup of parsley

4 Tablespoons of grainy mustard

2 Salmon filets (size your choice)

1 shallot

Directions:

1. First you finely chop the parsley and slice the shallots very thin.
2. After which, you spray or oil the baking sheet and lay the salmon filets on it.
3. After that, you squeeze or spoon about 2 tablespoons of mustard onto each piece of fish.
4. At this point, you evenly divide the parsley and shallots between them.
5. Then you bake at 350 for 15 minutes.
6. Finally, you serve with steamed asparagus and fresh squeezed lemon.

Pomegranate-Blueberry Baked Cod

Yield: 2 servings

things you will need*: measuring cups and spoons, baking sheet, knife, cutting board, mixing bowl, fork*

Ingredients:

½ cup of fresh blueberries

2/3-1 lb. of Cod

1 medium shallot

Coconut Oil

Freshly ground black pepper

1 lemon

1/3 cup of pomegranate seeds

Directions:

1. First, you heat oven to 350.
2. After which you spread a little coconut oil on a baking sheet and lay the cod on top.
3. After that, you rub some additional coconut oil onto the fish, and squeeze the juice of half the lemon over the top.
4. At this point, you finely chop the shallot.
5. Then in a small bowl, mash the blueberries.
6. Furthermore, you add the shallot, pomegranate seeds, fresh ground pepper and squeeze in the remaining half of the lemon juice.
7. After that, you spoon the mixture over the fish and bake for about 12-15 minutes.
8. Finally, you serve over a bed of steamed asparagus.

Pesto

Yield: 1/2 cup pesto (4 servings)
things you will need: *food processor or blender, measuring cups and spoons, mixing bowl, rubber spatula*

Ingredients:

2 Tablespoons of pine nuts

1-2 Tablespoons of fresh lemon juice, and rind for zesting

3-5 massive garlic cloves

Salt and pepper

½ cup of fresh spinach

1 cup plus or minus extra virgin cold-pressed olive oil

¾ cup of fresh basil

2 Tablespoons of walnuts

Directions:

1. First, you get out your food processor, and rinse and dry your basil and spinach.
2. After which you peel the garlic and mash it gently with the flat of a large knife.
3. Then when the greens are dry, put them in the blender and blend them in multiple quick, short pulses.
4. The trick here is not completely break them down but to get an even consistency.
5. Furthermore, you add the garlic and nuts and pulse again, scraping down the sides every few pulses to get the perfect mix.
6. After that, you pour the mixture into a bowl and begin adding olive oil, stirring it all together gently with a spatula.
7. At this point, you squeeze about 1-2 tablespoons of fresh lemon juice into the mixture.

8. Finally, you grate or zest some lemon rind – about ¼ teaspoon.

NOTE: make sure you taste it to see how much you like. Feel free to add a little salt and pepper to taste at this stage also.

CONCLUSION

Thanks for reading through this book; if you follow judiciously the recipes outlined above, you will improve your health, fight aging and lose excess weight without effort.

Remember, the only bad action you can take is no action at all.

www.ingramcontent.com/pod-product-compliance
Lightning Source LLC
Chambersburg PA
CBHW081725100526
44591CB00016B/2505